20 POP-UP CLASSROOM CARDS
For All Occasions!

Easy Reproducible Patterns for 3-D Cards
You and Your Students Make and Give

by Carmen R. Sorvillo

SCHOLASTIC
PROFESSIONAL **B**OOKS

New York • Toronto • London • Auckland • Sydney

Dedicated to Rose Sorvillo, my mother, who is never very far away.

Card patterns may be reproduced for classroom use. No other part of this publication may be reproduced in whole or in part, or stored in a retrieval system, or transmitted in any form or by any means, electronic, mechanical, photocopying, recording, or otherwise, without written permission of the publisher.
For information regarding permission, write to Scholastic Inc., 555 Broadway, New York, NY 10012

Illustration by Rusty Fletcher
Cover design by Jaime Lucero and Vincent Ceci
Interior design by Carmen R. Sorvillo

ISBN 0-590-55819-6

Copyright © 1998 by Scholastic. All rights reserved. Printed in the USA.

Contents

Introduction 4
Why Pop-Up Cards? 4
Tips for Making the Pop-Up Cards 5
Card-by-Card Directions 7

Holidays and Special Occasions

The First Day of School—Welcome Aboard! 15
Hip Hooray! Happy Birthday! 17
Happy Halloween! 19
Have a Great Thanksgiving Day! 21
Season's Greetings and a Happy New Year! 23
Today's the 100th Day of School! 25
It's Valentine's Day! 27
It's Earth Day! 29
Last Day of School Autograph Card 31

Celebrating Your Students

Congratulations, You're a Great Reader! 33
Write On! You're an Author! 35
Math Time! 37
You're a Super Scientist! 39
You've Lost a Tooth! 41
You're a Huge Success! 43
A Special Message 45
Thanks for Lending a Helping Hand! 47

Correspondence Home

A Very Special Invitation 49
We're Putting On a Special Show! 51
We're Sad to Hear That You Are Sick 53

Envelope Template 55

Introduction

My own interest in pop-ups stems from a childhood curiosity in how things worked. I always loved pressed-tin mechanical toys but they all had an inherent problem: They were passive entertainment. Long before such a toy saw the sun set in my care, I usually had ever so carefully taken it apart to examine its inner workings.

Pop-up storybooks ignited the same curiosity. I was totally delighted by them and fascinated by their seemingly magical ability to blossom like flowers before my eyes. An added source of wonder stemmed from my somehow providing the pop-ups' life force by simply opening the book and turning the pages. How was the motion of my hand mysteriously making inanimate drawings spring to life on the page?

It is my hope that these easy-to-make pop-up classroom cards will instill that kind of wonder and curiosity in your students—but at the very least, I'm sure that they will be a great deal of fun to both make and receive.

Why Pop-Up Cards?

The 20 reproducible pop-up classroom cards in this book can be used in a variety of ways:

● To Celebrate Special Days

Mark the first day of school, the last day of school, and all the special days in between by giving your students pop-up cards and by letting them make their own cards for friends and family.

● To Build the Home-School Connection

Capture parents' attention by sending home pop-up cards to announce a school play, an open house, or any other special event at your school.

● To Build Self-Esteem

Use a pop-up card to let students know that you are proud of a special achievement. A card from a teacher can be a great self-esteem booster for students.

● To Create a Learning Center or to Provide a Hands-On Class Project

Most of the cards in this book are designed to be simple enough for students to make themselves. Have plenty of cards on hand for students to make and decorate for friends and family. Making the holiday cards and invitation cards can be a great hands-on class project.

Tips for Making the Pop-Ups Cards

Copying the Pop-Up Cards

The pages in *Pop-Up Classroom Cards* are single-sided and perforated for easy removal and copying.

You can copy the cards on standard 8 1/2 " x 11" paper, which is easiest for children to work with. If you plan on cutting out the cards yourself, you might try using a slightly heavier stock paper (available from any office supply stores). It's harder to cut, but the stiffer paper will make a more durable card. You can also experiment by copying the cards on paper of different colors.

Cutting Out and Folding the Pop-Up Cards

The pop-ups in this book are variations of four basic constructions:

- **Horizontal box fold**
    Cards: The First Day of School—Welcome Aboard!
    Season's Greetings and a Happy New Year!
    Congratulations, You're a Great Reader!
    We're Putting On a Special Show!

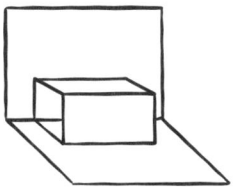

- **Vertical box fold**
    Cards: Have a Great Thanksgiving Day!
    Today's the 100th Day of School!
    Last Day of School Autograph Card
    Write On! You're an Author!
    You're a Super Scientist!
    You're a Huge Success!
    A Very Special Invitation
    We're Sad to Hear That You Are Sick

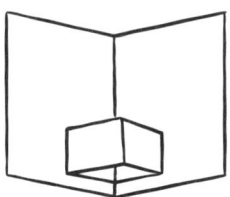

- **V-fold**
    Cards: Hip Hooray! Happy Birthday!
    It's Valentine's Day!
    It's Earth Day!
    Math Time!
    A Special Message
    Thanks for Lending a Helping Hand!

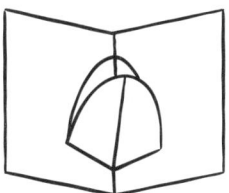

- **Double V-fold**
    Cards: Happy Halloween!
    You've Lost a Tooth!

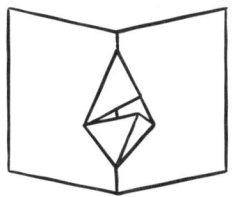

On all cards, the heavy solid lines are the cut lines. The dotted lines indicate ridge folds, which fold away from the card, and the dashed lines indicate valley folds.

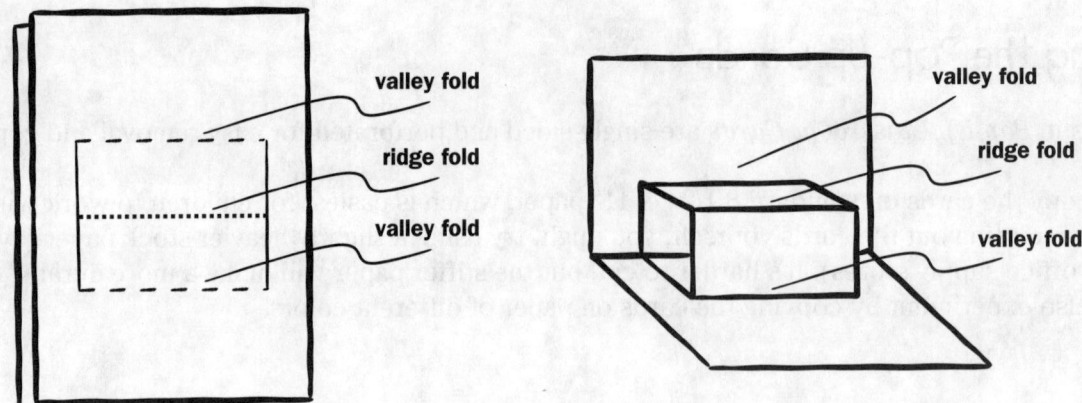

A craft knife is the easiest and quickest way for an adult to make the cards, but children can do well by poking a hole in the cut line and then cutting with safety scissors. If you're working with younger students, you might pre-cut the cards, then invite students to fold them.

When folding the cards, it's easiest to get a straight, neat fold by placing a ruler next to the fold line and making a crease along the edge of the ruler. A straight, well-creased fold is essential to the smooth operation of the pop-up.

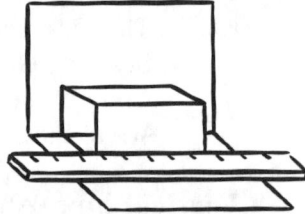

Use the template on page 55 to create envelopes for your pop-up cards.

Suggestions for Decorating the Pop-Up Cards

Be sure to allow your students time to color the cards. Coloring, however, need only be the beginning. To get you started, here are a few suggestions for decorating your cards.

- Add a festive touch to the birthday and invitation cards by gluing streamers and confetti to the cards.
- Try gluing small leaves to the cover of the Thanksgiving Day card or small decorative feathers to the turkey for an extra-special Thanksgiving card.
- Add silver glitter to the Season's Greetings card.
- Decorate the Valentine's Day card with scraps of ribbon and lace.
- Complement the Earth Day card by adding shiny star stickers to the inside.
- Enhance the underwater effect of the "Thank's for Lending a Helping Hand" card by gluing clear, blue, or green plastic wrap to the front of the card.

When adding any elements to the cards be sure to consider their effect on the opening and closing of the pop-up—and be careful not to glue the card closed.

After students have made several different cards, you might want to discuss with them the different types of pop-ups that they've made and help them understand how the cards work. Then encourage students to design and create their own pop-up cards.

Card-by-Card Directions

The First Day of School—Welcome Aboard!

What a great way to greet your new class! To help break the ice on the first day, invite students to spend a little time coloring their cards. You can also add a short note to parents on the inside of the card for students to take home.

page 15

1. Fold the paper in half horizontally along the dotted line. Then fold it in half again so that "The first day of school" is on the cover and "Welcome aboard!" is on the inside of the card.
2. Unfold the paper. Then cut along the two vertical solid lines on each side of the bus. Refold the paper to form the card.
3. Open the card to reveal the pop-up. Pull the pop-up out and make a crease along the horizontal dashed lines at the top and bottom of the pop-up to create two valley folds.
4. Make a crease along the horizontal dotted line in the center of the pop-up to form a ridge fold.
5. Close the card and reopen it to see the school bus pop up.

page 17

Hip Hooray! Happy Birthday!

Make a personalized birthday card by writing the birthday boy or girl's name and age on the cover. There's room inside for everyone to sign.

1. Fold the paper in half horizontally along the dotted line. Then fold it in half again so that "Hip Hooray!" is on the cover and "Happy Birthday!" is on the inside of the card.
2. Unfold and hold the paper so that "Happy Birthday!" is right-side up. Following the solid line, cut around the birthday cake. Then refold the paper to form the card.
3. Open the card to reveal the pop-up. Pull the pop-up out and make a crease along each of the slanted dashed lines to create two valley folds.
4. Crease along the vertical dotted line in the center of the pop-up to form a ridge fold.
5. Close the card and reopen it to see the birthday cake pop up.
6. Cut out as many candles (page 18) as needed and glue them to the birthday cake.

Happy Halloween!

The opening and closing mouth in this pop-up card is sure to delight your students!

page 19

1. Fold the paper in half horizontally along the dotted line. Then fold it in half again so that "On Halloween, Know what we do?" is on the cover and "Boooooooo!" is on the inside of the card.
2. Unfold the paper. Then cut along the horizontal solid line in the center of the pop-up. Refold the paper to form the card.

3. Open the card and push the pop-up out. Then make a crease along each of the dashed lines to create four valley folds.
4. Crease along the vertical dotted line in the center of the pop-up to form a ridge fold.
5. Close the card and reopen it to see the child's mouth open and close.

Have a Great Thanksgiving Day!

page 21

Your students will love to give and receive these adorable Thanksgiving Day cards that feature a pop-up turkey!

1. Fold the paper in half horizontally along the dotted line, keeping the printed side showing.
2. Unfold the paper. Starting at the top of the vertical dashed line on the left side of the pop-up, cut around the edge of the turkey. Continue cutting along the solid horizontal line on the right side of the turkey. Finally, cut along the horizontal solid line at the bottom of the pop-up.
3. Pull the pop-up out and make a crease along the vertical dashed lines on each side of the pop-up to create two valley folds.
4. Refold the paper in half horizontally. Then—being careful not to fold the turkey—fold the paper in half again to create a ridge fold along the vertical dotted line in the center of the pop-up base.
5. Open the card to see the turkey pop up.

Season's Greetings and a Happy New Year!

This pop-up snowman card is perfect for teachers and students to make at holiday time.

page 23

1. Fold the paper in half horizontally along the dotted line, keeping the printed side showing.
2. Unfold the paper and cut along the two vertical solid lines on each side of the snowman. Then, starting at the end of the horizontal dotted line and following the solid line, cut around the top of the snowman. Stop cutting when you reach the horizontal dotted line on the other side.
3. Refold the paper in half horizontally. Then pull the pop-up out by sliding both thumbs under the center area. Next, make a crease along the horizontal dashed lines at the top and bottom of the snowman to create two valley folds.
4. Crease along the short horizontal dotted lines on each side of the snowman to form a ridge fold. Then—being careful not to fold the top of the snowman—fold the card in half again.
5. Close the card and reopen it to see the snowman pop up.

page 25

Today's the 100th Day of School!

Initiate a surprise celebration on the 100th day of school by tying "100th Day of School" cards to helium-filled balloons. Then anchor a balloon and a card to each student's desk.

1. Fold the paper in half horizontally along the dotted line. Then fold in half again, so that "I'm here to tell you something cool," is on the front cover and "Today's the 100th day of school!" is on the inside of the card.
2. Unfold the paper. Then cut along the three horizontal solid lines. Refold the paper to form the card.
3. Open the card to reveal the two pop-ups. Pull the pop-ups out and make a crease along each of the vertical dashed lines to create four valley folds.
4. Crease along the vertical dotted lines in the center of both pop-ups to form ridge folds.
5. Close the card and reopen it to see the two sections of balloons pop up.

It's Valentine's Day!

Everyone loves to get a Valentine! Let your students make these cards for their friends and family.

page 27

1. Fold the paper in half horizontally along the dotted line. Then fold it in half again so that "It's Valentine's Day!" is on the cover and "Please be my Valentine!" is on the inside of the card.
2. Unfold the paper. Then, starting at the top of the slanted dashed line on one side, cut along the solid line around the heart until you reach the slanted dashed line on the other side. Refold the paper to form the card.
3. Open the card to reveal the pop-up. Pull the pop-up out and make a crease along each of the slanted dashed lines to create two valley folds.
4. Crease along the vertical dotted line in the center of the pop-up to form a ridge fold.
5. Close the card and reopen it to see the heart pop up.

page 29

It's Earth Day!

Give your Earth Day science lesson the added punch of a pop-up-card project!

1. Fold the paper in half horizontally along the dotted line. Then fold it in half again so that "Water and air With the animals We share—" is on the cover and "It's Earth Day! " is on the inside of the card.
2. Unfold the paper. Then, starting at the top of the slanted dashed line on one side, cut around the earth, following the solid line, until you reach the dashed line on the other side. Refold the paper to form the card.

3. Open the card to reveal the pop-up. Pull the pop-up out and make a crease along each of the slanted dashed lines, creating two valley folds.
4. Crease along the vertical dotted line in the center of the pop-up to form a ridge fold.
5. Close the card and reopen it to see the earth pop up.

Last Day of School Autograph Card

Your students will love making these pop-up autograph cards on the last day of school. Have plenty of red, green, yellow, and blue colored pencils on hand for an autograph party.

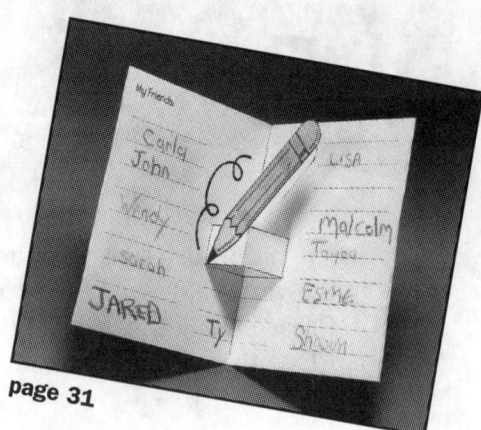
page 31

1. Fold the paper in half horizontally along the dotted line, keeping the printed side showing.
2. Unfold the paper and cut along the horizontal solid line underneath the pencil. Next, cut along the horizontal solid line to the left of the pencil. Continue cutting around the pencil and across the solid horizontal line on right side of the pencil.
3. Pull the pop-up out and make a crease along the vertical dashed lines on each side of the pop-up to create two valley folds.
4. Fold the paper in half again. Then—being careful not to fold the pencil—fold the paper in half again to create a ridge fold along the vertical dotted line in the center of the pop-up.
5. Open the card to see the pencil pop up.

Congratulations, You're a Great Reader!

Watch your young readers' eyes pop when they open these cards and see the pop-up storybook castle!

page 33

1. Fold the paper in half horizontally along the dotted line.
2. Unfold the paper and cut along the two vertical solid lines on each side of the castle. Then, following the solid line, cut around the top part of the castle, starting at the horizontal dotted line on one side of the castle and stopping at the horizontal dotted line on the other side.
3. Fold the card in half again. Pull the pop-up out and make a crease along the horizontal dashed lines at the top and bottom of the pop-up, creating two valley folds.
4. Crease along the two horizontal dotted lines on each side of the castle to form a ridge fold.
5. Fold the card in half again—being careful not to fold the top of the castle.
6. Open the card to see the castle pop-up.

Write On! You're an Author!

Use these cards to celebrate your young authors—and encourage them to keep writing!

1. Fold the paper in half horizontally along the dotted line. Then fold it in half again so that "I'm sending you This little note…" is on the cover and "Write On!" is on the inside of the card.
2. Unfold the paper. Then cut along the two horizontal solid lines above and the below the pop-up. Refold the paper to form the card.
3. Open the card. Pull the pop-up out and make a crease along the each of the vertical dashed lines, creating two valley folds.
4. Crease along the vertical dotted line in the center of the pop-up to form a ridge fold.
5. Close the card and reopen it to see the book pop-up.

page 35

Math Time!

page 37

This interactive card, which features movable hour and minute clock hands, makes a wonderful tie-in to a math lesson on telling time.

1. Fold the paper in half horizontally along the dotted line. Then fold it in half again so that "2, 4, 6, 8…" is on the cover and "You do just great!" is on the inside of the card.
2. Unfold the paper. Then, starting at the end of one of the dashed lines, cut along the solid line around the edge of the clock. Stop when you reach the dashed line on the other side. Refold the paper to form the card.
3. Open the card to reveal the pop-up. Pull the pop-up out and make a crease along each of the slanted dashed lines to create two valley folds.
4. Crease along the vertical dotted line in the center of the pop-up to form a ridge fold.
5. Close the card and reopen it to see the clock pop up.
6. Cut out the hour and minute hands on page 38, and attach them to the center of the clock with a brass paper fastener. The card will fold best if you position the two fastener ends vertically and the two clock hands horizontally.

You're a Super Scientist!

Reward a student who has a special interest in science with this card. The center of the magnifying glass can be left solid, or you can cut it out and actually see the bug through the magnifying glass!

1. Fold the paper in half horizontally along the dotted line, keeping the printed side showing.
2. Unfold and hold the paper so that "You're a super scientist!" is right-side-up. Cut along the horizontal solid line at the top of the pop up. Following the solid line, continue to cut around the magnifying glass and thumb, stopping at the vertical dashed line on the right.

page 39

Next, cut along the horizontal solid line at the bottom of the pop-up. You can also cut out the center of the magnifying glass.
3. Make a crease along the vertical dashed lines on each side of the pop-up to create two valley folds.
4. Refold the paper in half horizontally. Then—being careful not to fold the magnifying glass—fold the paper in half again to create a ridge fold along the vertical dotted line in the center of the pop-up.
5. Open the card to see the magnifying glass pop up.

You've Lost a Tooth!

Don't let an important rite of passage slip by unnoticed! Whenever a student loses a tooth, use this card to celebrate his or her "growing up."

page 41

1. Fold the paper in half horizontally along the dotted line. Then fold it in half again so that "You must be 'beary' proud." on the cover and "You've lost a tooth, so shout out loud!" is on the inside of the card.
2. Unfold the paper. Then cut along the horizontal solid line in the center of the bear's mouth. Also cut out the small black missing tooth in the bear's mouth. Refold the paper to form the card.
3. Open the card to reveal the pop-up. Push the pop-up out and make a crease along each of the slanted dashed lines to create four valley folds.
4. Crease along the vertical dotted line in the center of the pop-up to form a ridge fold.
5. Close the card and reopen it to see the bear's mouth open and close.

You're a Huge Success!

This lovable dinosaur pop-up card is a great way to encourage academic excellence and build self-esteem!

page 43

1. Fold the paper in half horizontally along the dotted line, keeping the printed side showing.
2. Unfold and hold the paper so that "You're a huge success!" is right-side-up. Cut along the horizontal solid line at the bottom of the pop-up. Then, starting at the top of the dashed line on the left, cut along the solid line around the dinosaur's head. Continue cutting along the horizontal solid line to the right of the dinosaur.
3. Pull the pop-up out and make a crease along the vertical dashed lines on each side of the pop-up to create two valley folds.
4. Refold the paper in half horizontally. Then—being careful not to fold the dinosaur's head—fold the paper in half again to create a ridge fold along the vertical dotted line in the center of the pop-up.
5. Open the card to see the dinosaur pop up.

page 45

A Special Message

This card is perfect for any occasion. You can also use it to jump-start a class activity by writing a story starter on the pop-up.

1. Fold the paper in half horizontally along the dotted line. Then fold it in half again so that "A special message just for you..." on the cover and "A plain old note..." is on the inside of the card.
2. Unfold and hold the paper so that "A plain old note just wouldn't do" is right-side-up. Cut along the solid lines on the left, top, and right side of the note. Refold the paper to form the card.
3. Open the card to reveal the pop-up. Pull the pop-up out and make a crease along both of the slanted dashed lines to create two valley folds.
4. Crease along the dotted line in the center of the pop-up to form a ridge fold.
5. Close the card and reopen it to see the note pop up.

Thanks for Lending a Helping Hand!

Let your students know how much their help around the classroom is appreciated with this fun thank you card!

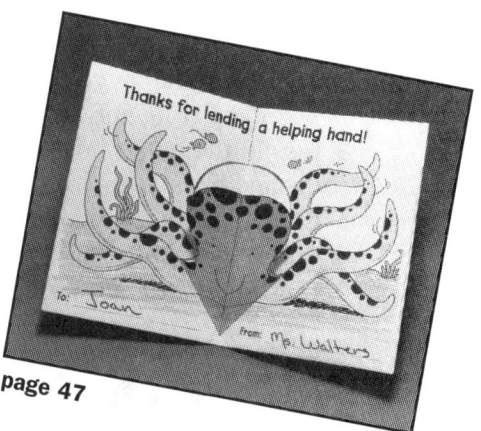
page 47

1. Fold the paper in half horizontally along the dotted line. Then fold it in half again so that "You're the one I think is grand!" is on the cover and "Thanks for lending a helping hand!" is on the inside of the card.
2. Unfold the paper. Then, starting at the top of the dashed line on one side, cut around the octopus' head. Stop when you reach the end of the dashed line on the other side. Refold the paper to form the card.
3. Open the card to reveal the pop-up. Pull the pop-up out and make a crease along both of the slanted dashed lines to create two valley folds.
4. Crease along the dotted line in the center of the pop-up to form a ridge fold.
5. Close the card and reopen it to see the octopus pop up.

A Very Special Invitation

Create these cards as a class project before your next open house or other special school-event. Write the name of the event on the pop-up banner.

page 49

1. Fold the paper in half horizontally along the dotted line. Then fold it in half again so that "A Very Special Invitation from ____" is on the cover and "Please come to our ____!" is on the inside of the card.
2. Unfold the paper. Then cut along the two horizontal solid lines above and below the banner. Refold the paper to form the card.

3. Open the card and pull the pop-up out. Then, make a crease along the vertical dashed lines on each side of the pop-up to create two valley folds.
4. Make a crease along the dotted line in the center of the pop-up to form a ridge fold.
5. Close the card and reopen to see the banner pop-up.

We're Putting on a Special Show!

Parents will love receiving these special invitations—and making the cards can be a great way to get the whole class involved in the play! Students can fill in the place, date, and time and then write the title of the production on the marquee!

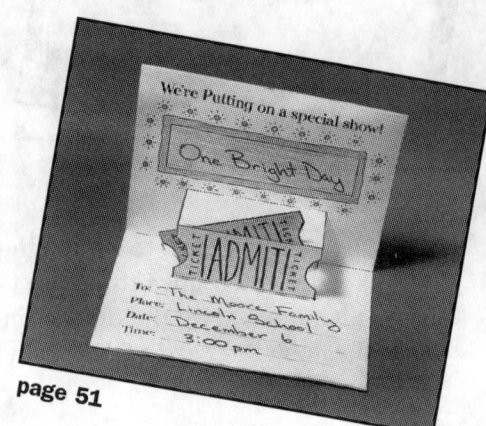
page 51

1. Fold the paper in half horizontally along the dotted line, keeping the printed side showing.
2. Unfold and hold the paper so that "We're Putting on a Special Show!" is right-side-up. First, cut along the two vertical solid lines on the outside edge of the tickets. Next, cut around the corner of the rear ticket, starting and stopping the dotted lines.
3. Refold the paper horizontally and pull the pop-up out. Then, make a crease along the horizontal dashed lines at the top and bottom of the pop-up to create two valley folds.
4. Crease along the two horizontal dotted lines in the middle of the pop-up to form a ridge fold.
5. Carefully fold the card in half again, making sure not to fold the top corner of the rear ticket.
6. Close the card and reopen it to see the tickets pop up.

page 53

We're Sad to Hear That You Are Sick

Let students who are sick know that everyone at school misses them. Be sure to add the student's name to the pop-up banner. You can make one card for all the class to sign or have each student make a card.

1. Fold the paper in half horizontally along the dotted line. Then fold it in half again, so that "We're sad to hear that you are sick." is on the front cover and "We hope you're better super quick!" is on the inside of the card.
2. Unfold the paper. Then cut along the two horizontal solid lines above and below the banner. Refold the paper to form the card.
3. Open the card to reveal the pop-up. Pull the pop-up out and make a crease along each of the vertical dashed lines to create two valley folds.
4. Make a crease along the dotted line in the center of the pop-up to form a ridge fold.
5. Close the card and reopen it to see the sign pop up.

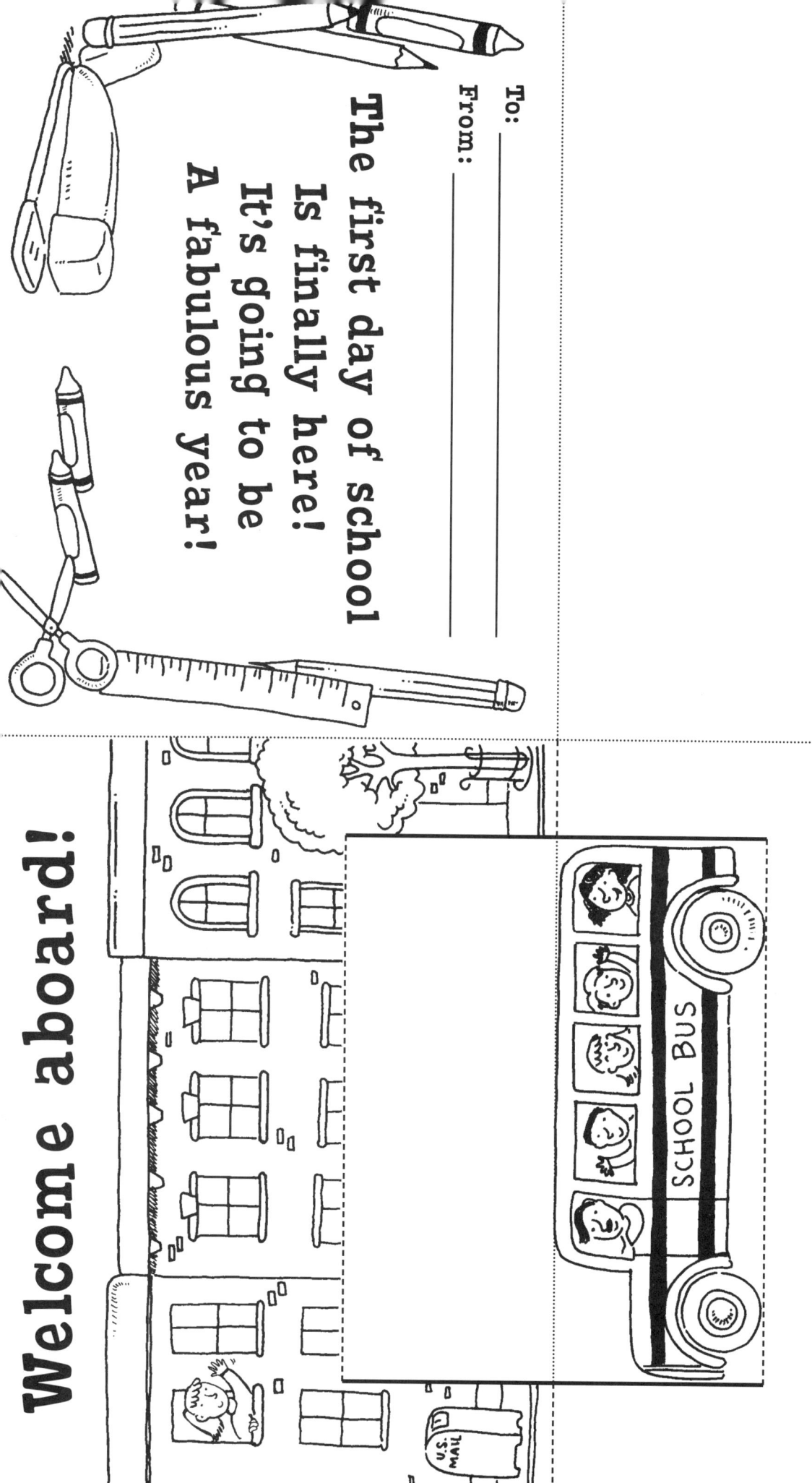

Welcome aboard!

To: _____
From: _____

The first day of school
Is finally here!
It's going to be
A fabulous year!

Hip Hooray!

_____ is
___ years old
today!

Happy Birthday!

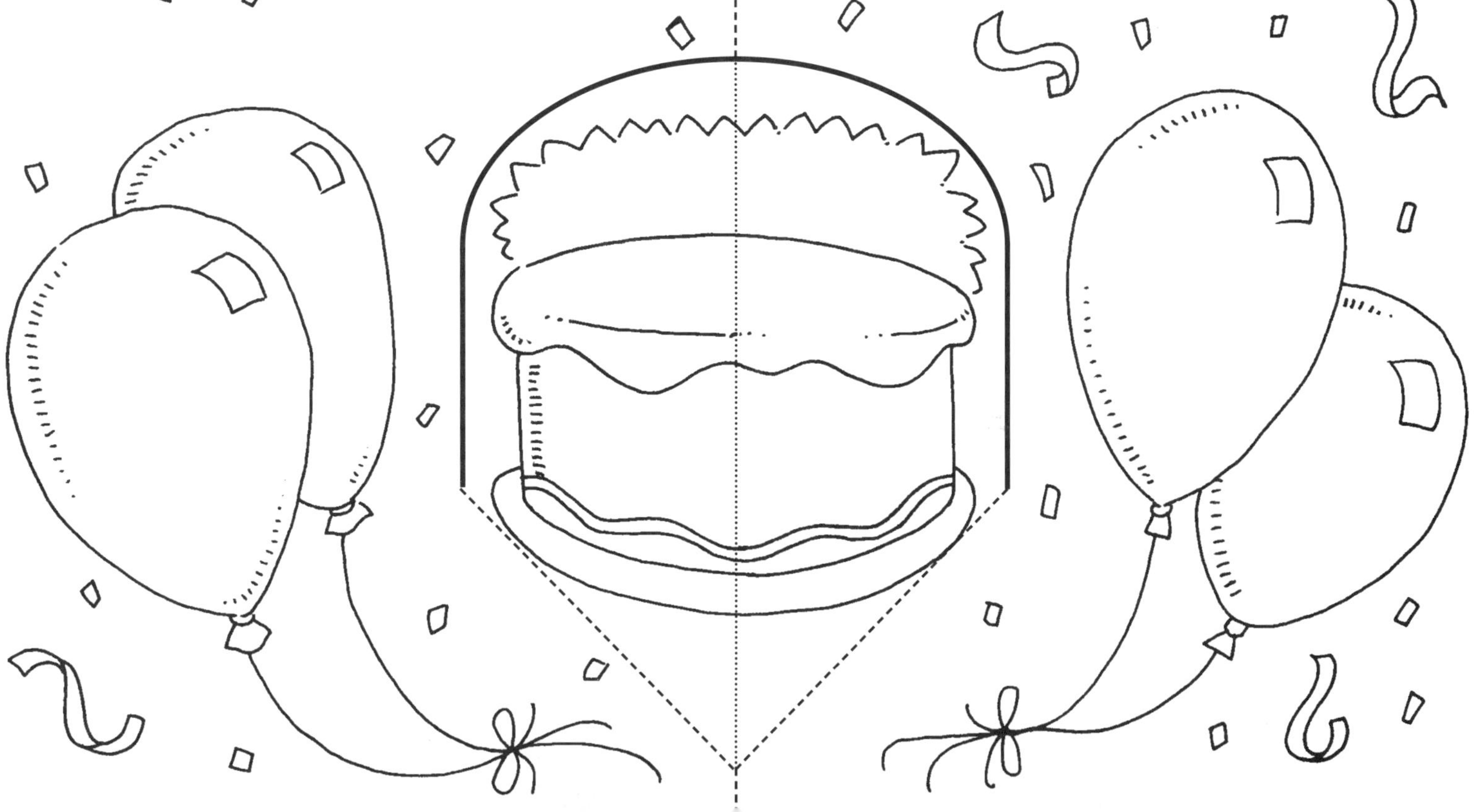

Birthday Candles

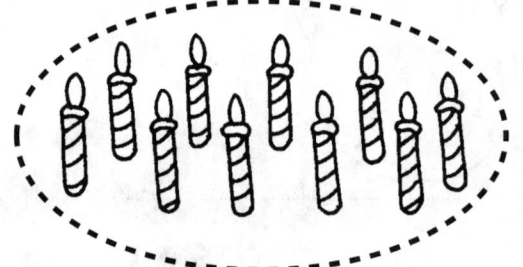

Cut out the birthday candles, trimming off unneeded candles from the ends. Glue the candles onto the birthday cake.

On Halloween,
We all shout...

On Halloween,
know what we do?

"Booooo oooo!"

Happy Halloween!

To: _____ From: _____

I'm here to tell you something cool...

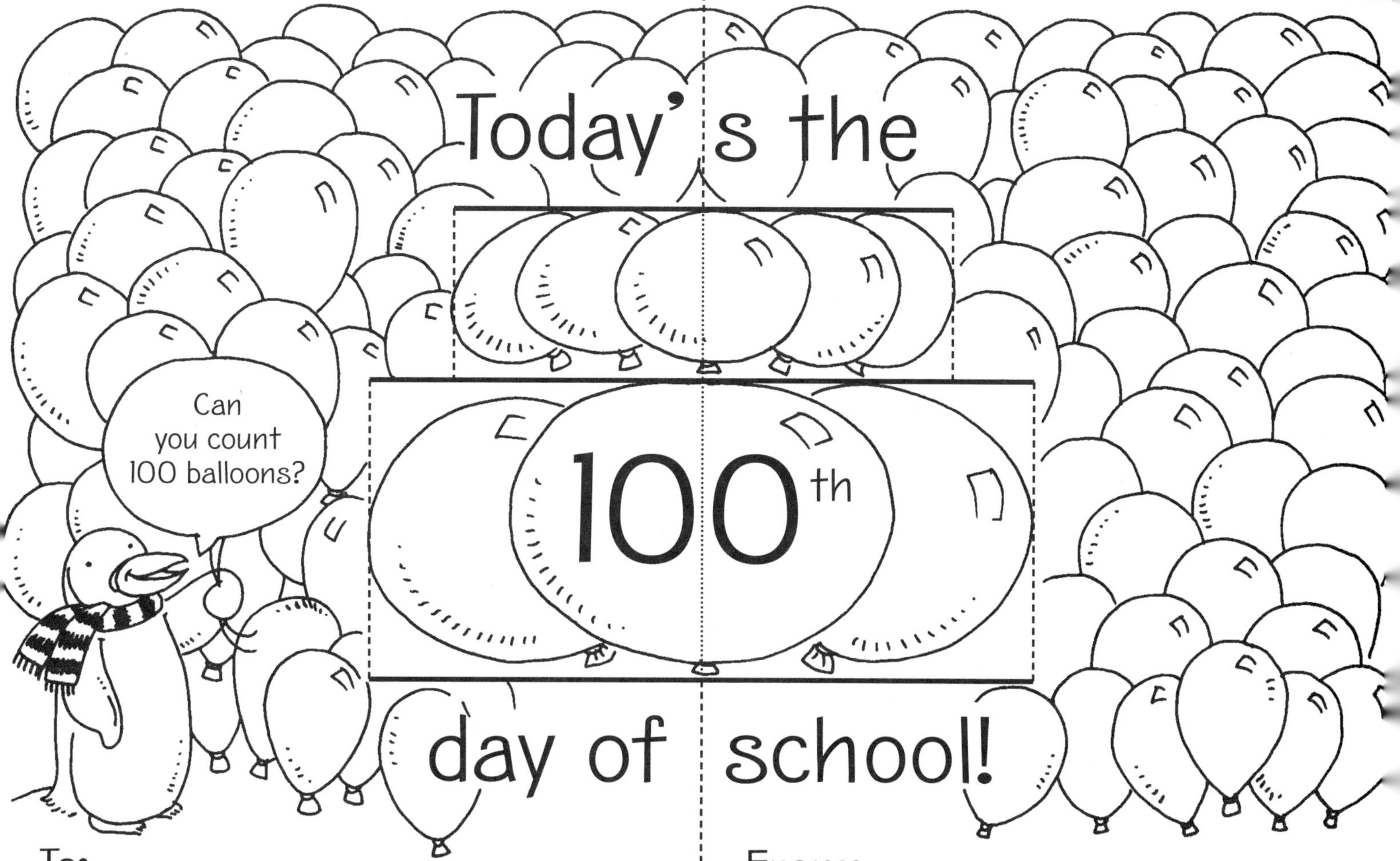

Today's the 100th day of school!

Can you count 100 balloons?

To: _____ From: _____

It's Valentine's Day!

I hope, I hope, You'll be my

I hope, you'll say... Valentine today!

Please be my Valentine!

To: _____

From: _____

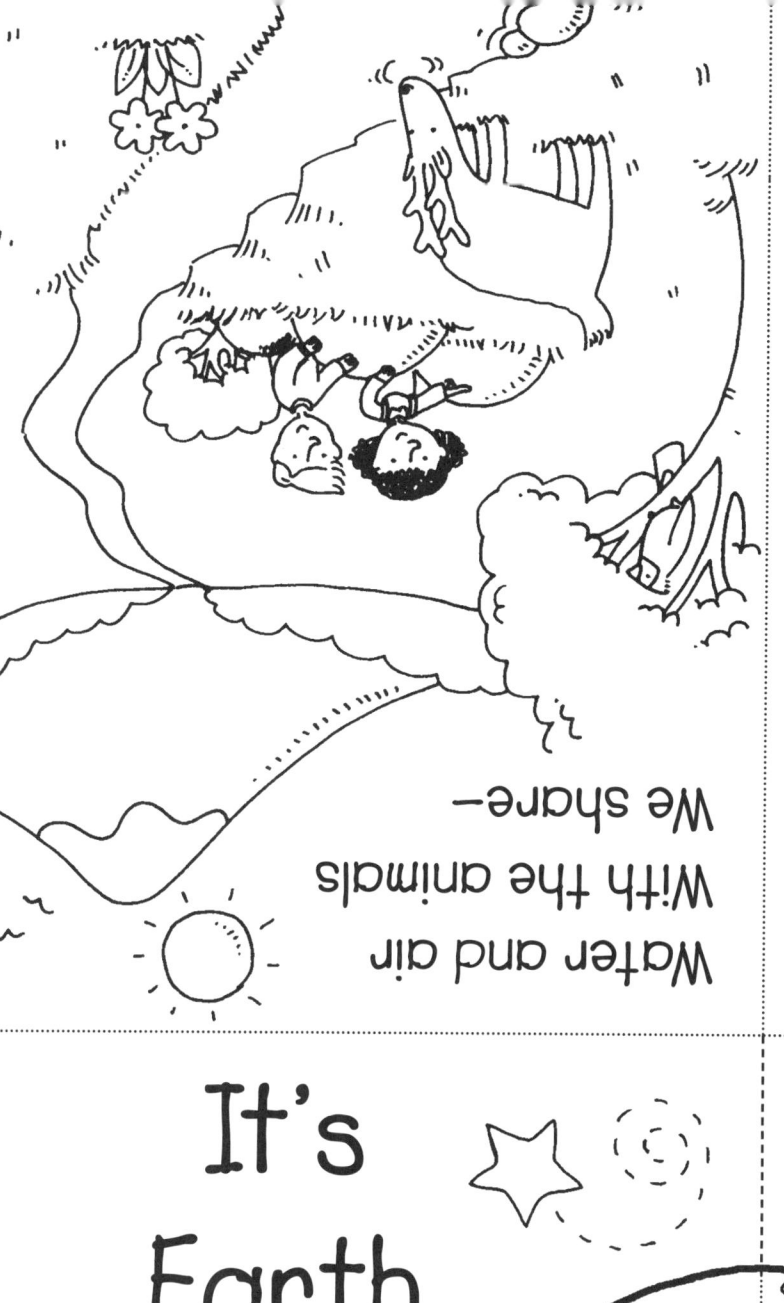

Water and air
With the animals
We share—

It's
Earth
Day!

Let's show
we care!

To: _____   From: _____

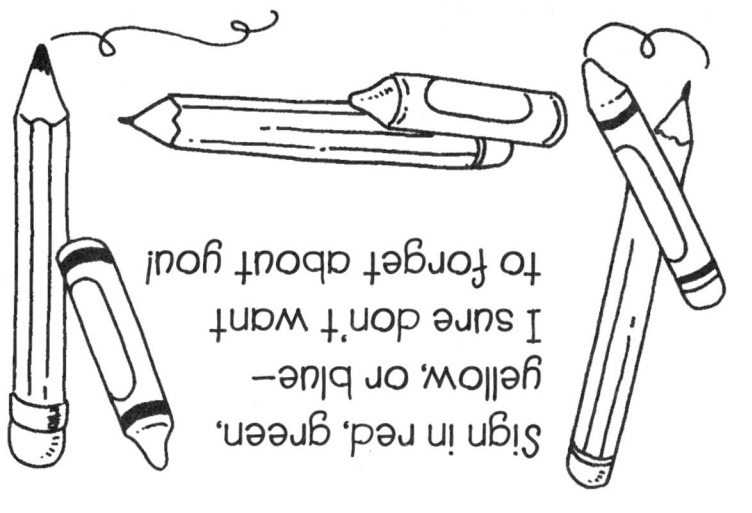

Autograph Card

Sign in red, green, yellow, or blue—
I sure don't want to forget about you!

My Name: _____

My Teacher: _____

Date: _____ Grade: _____

My Friends:

_____
_____
_____
_____
_____
_____
_____
_____

_____
_____
_____
_____
_____
_____
_____
_____

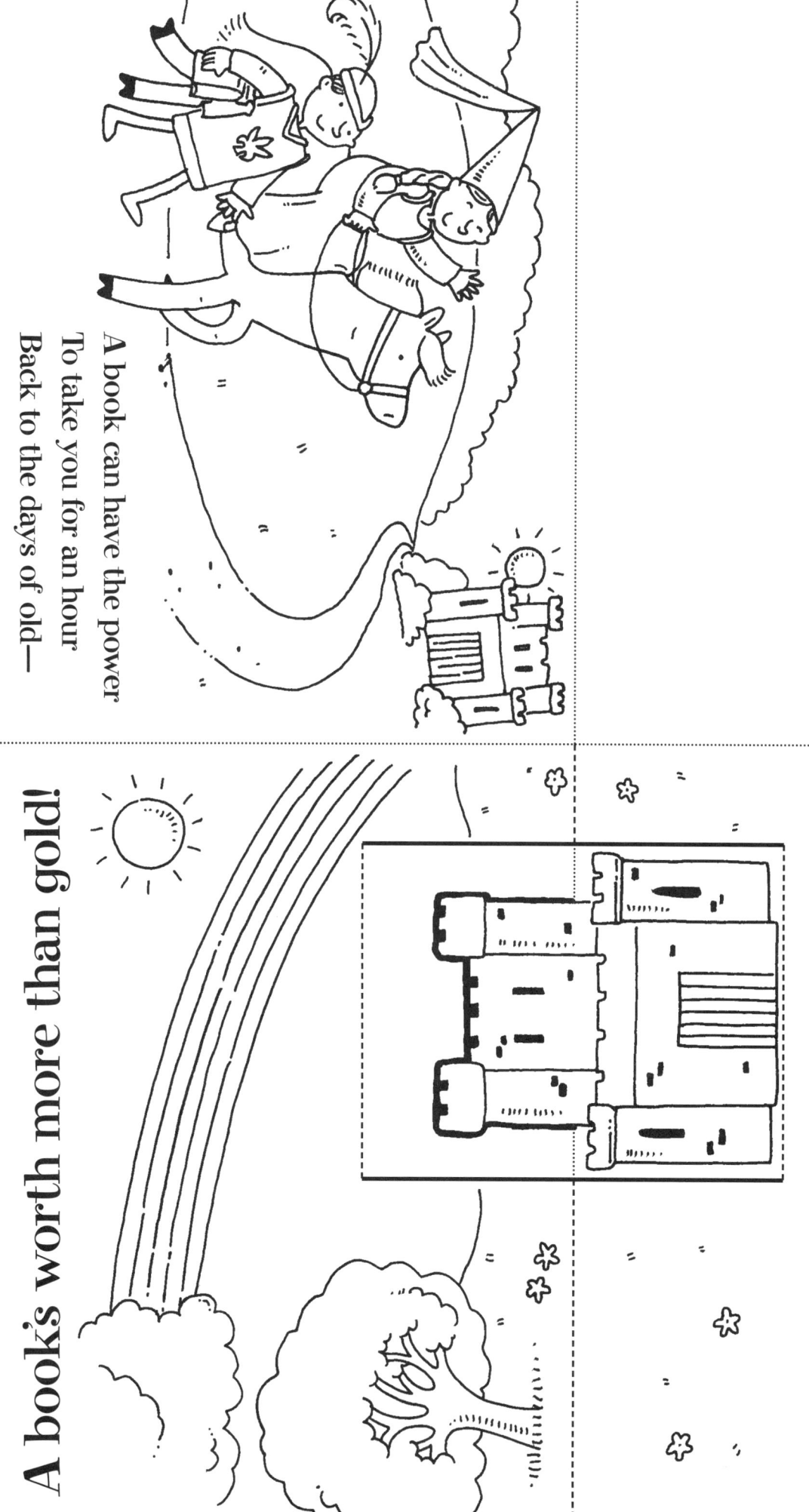

A book can have the power
To take you for an hour
Back to the days of old—

A book's worth more than gold!

Congratulations, _____.

You're a great reader!

I'm sending you
This little note
To say I'm proud
Of what you wrote!

Write on!

```
_____

        b y

_____
```

You're an author!

To: _____   From: _____

When it's time for math,

You do just great!

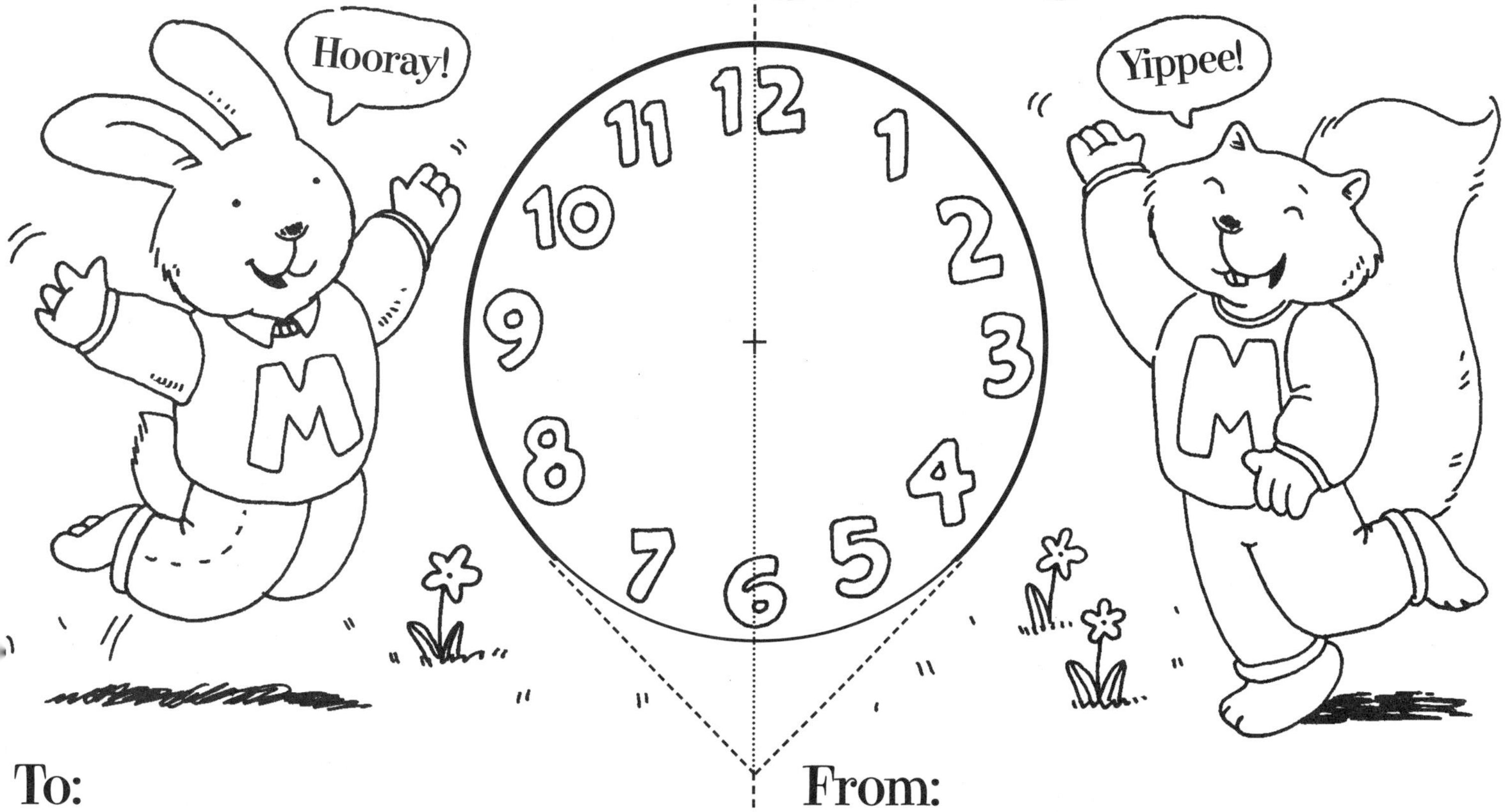

Hooray!

Yippee!

To: _____

From: _____

Clock Hands

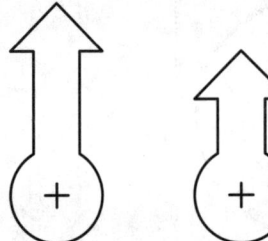

Cut out each hand of the clock. Cut the crossed lines at the round end of each hand and in the center of the clock. Push a brass fastener through the hour hand, the minute hand and then the center of the clock. Flatten the back of the fastener and turn the ends so that they will be in the vertical crease of the card when folded.

I have to say, I can't resist...

You're a super scientist!

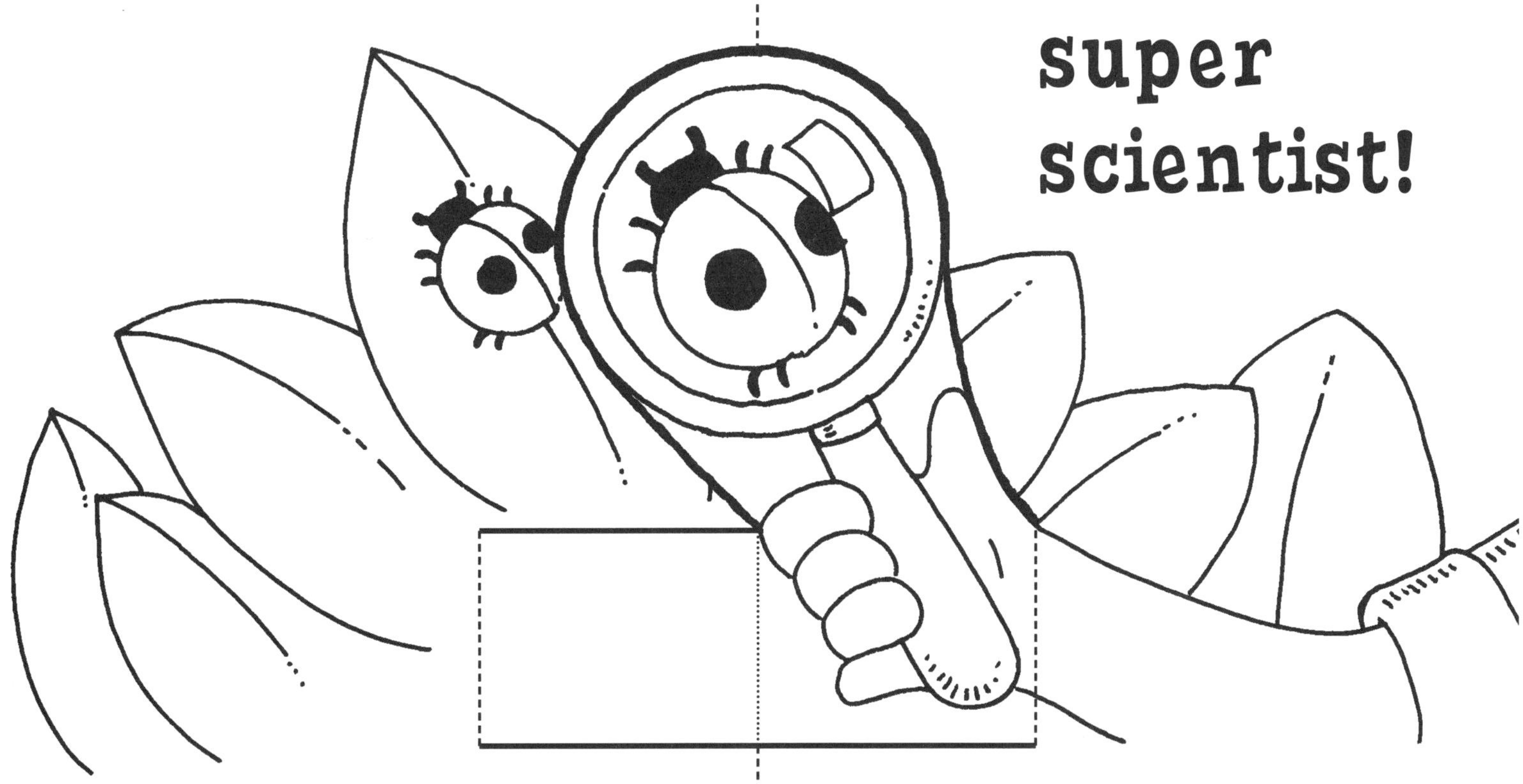

To: _____ From: _____

You must be "beary" proud.

You've lost a tooth, so shout out loud!

To: _____

From: _____

keep up the
good work.

You're a huge success!

To: _____ From: _____

A special message just for you...

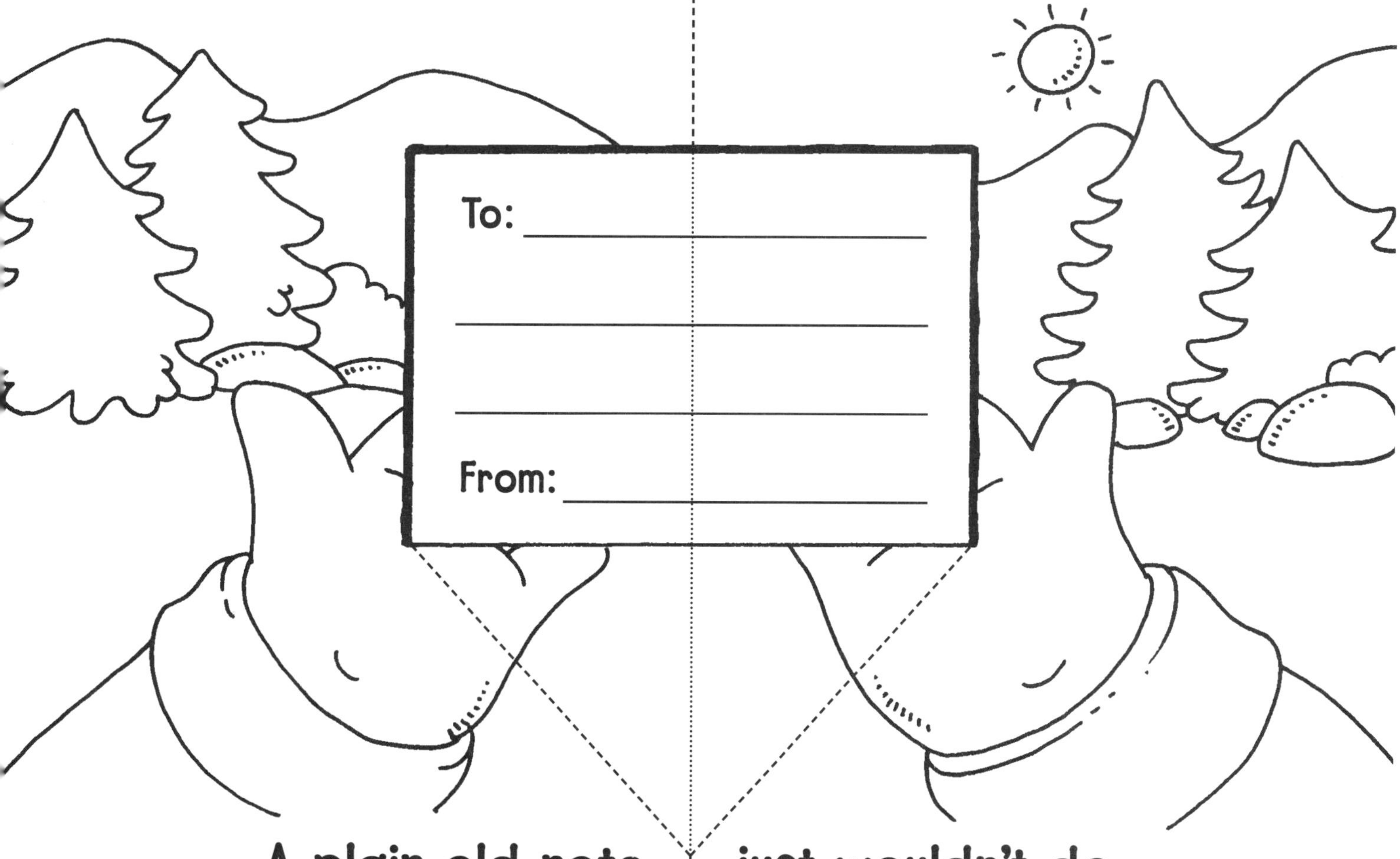

A plain old note just wouldn't do.

You're the one
I think is grand!

Thanks for lending a helping hand!

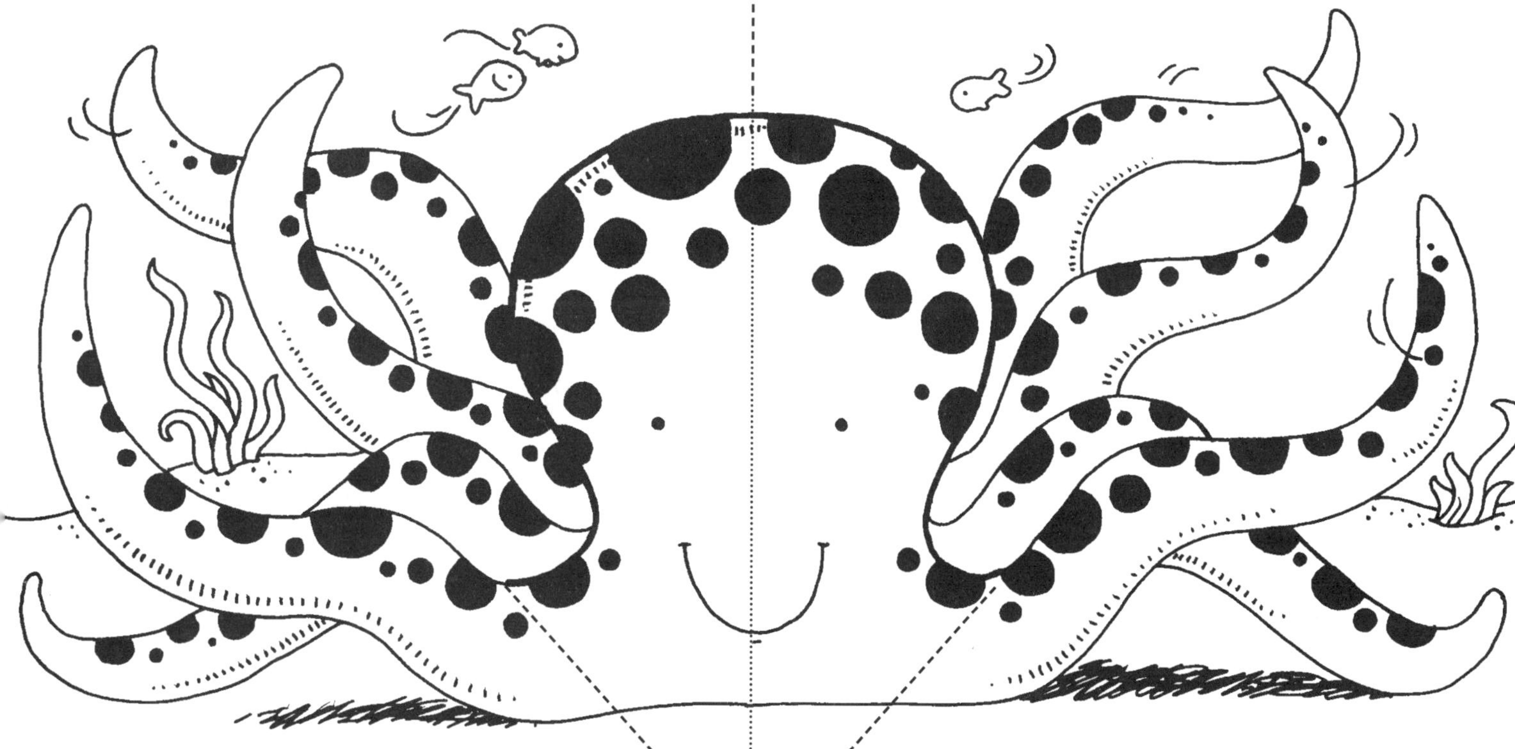

To: _____

From: _____

A very special
invitation from

Please come
to our

To: _____
Place: _____

Date: _____
Time: _____

We're sad to hear that you are sick.

We hope you're better super quick!

We miss you, _____!

Envelope Pattern

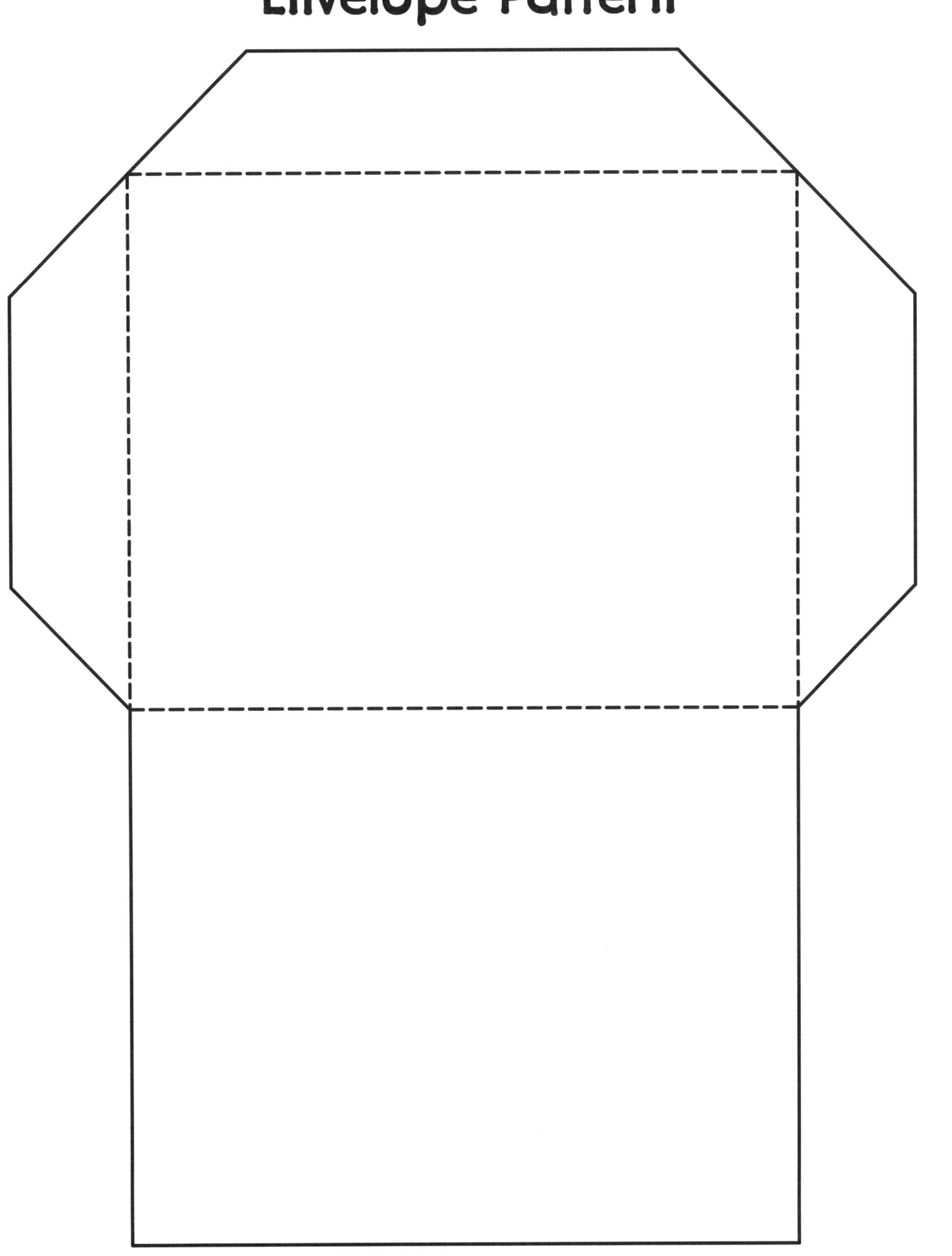

Envelope Directions

1. Photocopy the envelope pattern on page 55.
2. Cut the pattern along the solid lines.
3. Fold the pattern along the dashed lines.
4. Paste or tape the side flaps.
5. Insert your folded classroom card and seal.

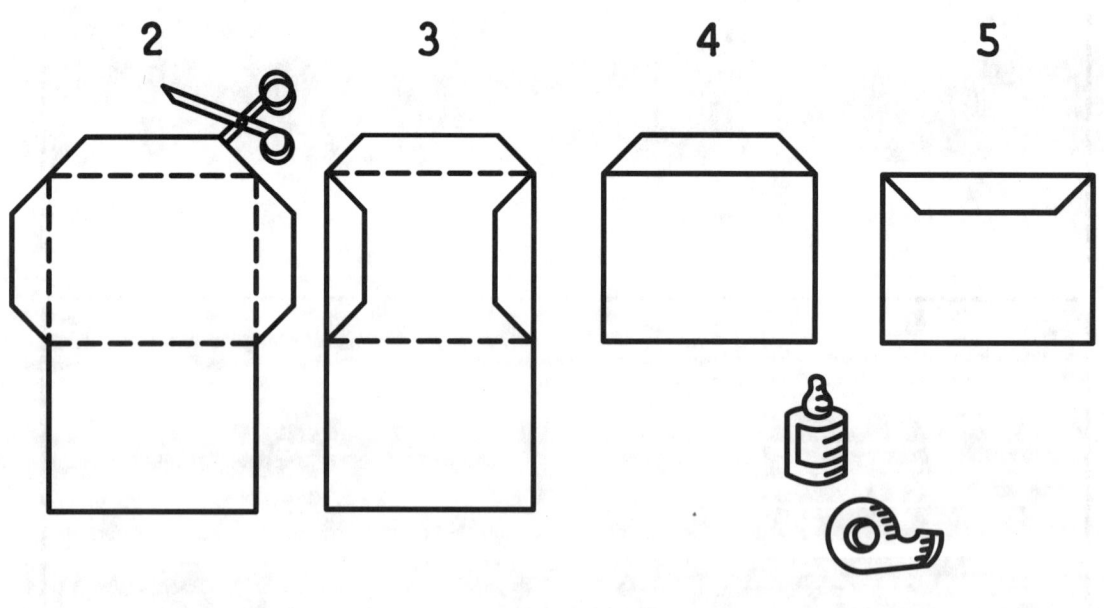